Whispered Wisdom

WHISPERED WISDOM
To Live Beyond

Terry Hoggard

WHISPERED WISDOM TO LIVE BEYOND

ISBN 978-0692417966

Cover and interior design by truenorthpublish.com.

Send corrections to brian@truenorthpublish.com.

For worldwide distribution. Printed in the United States of America.

Table of Contents

Preface

I have to admit that seeing my name attached to a book seems beyond the realm of possibility. It is definitely beyond my capacity, but this project perfectly illustrates three of the great life lessons I have learned.

◊ *Never live at the level of your possibility, but reach for His fullest potential.*

◊ *When taking on a task that is bigger than you, pray first and then build a team.*

◊ *Focusing on your minimum will stop you from ever experiencing His maximum, so look and live beyond.*

I am grateful that these lessons have been powerfully released in my life and that I have been blessed with family and friends who have faithfully reinforced these realities to me. While there would be too many to mention by name, every one of them has been written on my heart.

When I began to create my quotes and sayings I chose to use the word "ascolta" as my tag line ... "ascolta" is an Italian word meaning "listen, pay attention, be attentive." My term "Whispered Wisdom" comes from this connection.

This book, Whispered Wisdom to Live Beyond, is a collection of these quotes and sayings, created with the hope they will inspire, encourage and provoke those who read them to choose to live beyond themselves ... fully committed to making a difference.

As you read, this remains my simple desire.

Terry Hoggard

Special Thanks

I am eternally grateful to God who has transformed my life, taken me to places that I never dreamed I would go, allowed me to do things I never imagined that I would do, to develop the most amazing friendships and taught me how to live beyond my limited possibilities by entering into His limitless potential. What a God!

I want to express my deepest gratitude to my wife Ruthanne and my daughters Kari and Kristi who have openly shared all of life with me. To Andrew, my son-in-law and the three beautiful grandchildren (Caleb, Luke and Hannah) that he and Kristi have added to our family. Each of them motivate me to "live beyond" and I am better in every way because of them!

To the Filipino churches and individuals of Bologna, Empoli, Florence, Livorno, Pisa (ADIMEF REGION III) who generously provided the financial support to launch this project.

Special thanks to Brian Del Turco who invested himself in this project doing the book shaping work, interior design, layout, cover design, and product placement. There is no doubt that he took me beyond my capacity. Brian is a family member with whom I now share a very special bond. Thank you friend!

The City of Rome

ROME ... our original "destination" city!

We arrived there on June 17, 1986, direct from Kansas with our two little girls, 17 checked bags, 4 carry-ons and 4 Cabbage Patch dolls in tow.

We must have been quite a sight!

From those humble beginnings, we began what was an entirely unknown missionary journey that utterly transformed our lives. Almost 10 years of ministry in the city and the nation resulted in the birthing of new churches and ministry initiatives, as well as the building of lifelong friendships that continue to thrive in every way.

I will always have a deep affection for and an attraction to Rome. It was there that my faith was stirred, my heart was changed and my life calling was nurtured and developed.

ROME ... a beautiful city, with beautiful people and a spiritual destiny that remains broken, and yet yearns to be fulfilled.

Terry Hoggard

(Rome, Italy is shown on the cover and chapter title pages of 'Whispered Wisdom to Live Beyond.')

THE PRIORITY OF

*"Keep adding value to your relationships ...
each one is a treasure!"*
— Terry

The quality of our relationships makes all the difference in our lives ... in our place in the world.

Think of it! When the fellowship of the Godhead—Father, Son, and Holy Spirit—desired to create humanity, placing the very image of God in the earth, a family was created.

Then God said, "Let us make man in our image, in our likeness, and let them rule" ... So God created man in his own image, in the image of God he created him: male and female he created them. God blessed them and said to them, "Be fruitful and increase in number; fill the earth and subdue it" (Genesis 1:26-28).

Human relationships were created by divine relationship. The Creator is *highly relational!* If we undervalue this, we weaken our lives.

Whether we're considering a biological family, or any setting or context, relational life is paramount! You can confidently say that things rise or fall on the principle of relationships.

Jesus reduced everything to love and relational integrity—*"Love the Lord your God with all your heart and with all your soul and with all your mind. This is the first and greatest commandment. And the second is like it: Love your neighbor as yourself. All the Law and the Prophets hang on these two commandments"* (Matthew 22:37-40).

Let's prioritize relationships and see if our life experience is elevated! I believe we'll be more than happy with the outcome.

Pour on the Value!

Keep adding value to your relationships ...

> *and yes, it is a lifelong commitment!*
> *truly a gift that keeps on giving!*
> *each one is a treasure!*
> *the payback is powerful!*
> *every shared moment creates a special memory!*
> *they will be life-giving streams!*
> *it is a worthy investment!*

Pay Attention to Those Closest to You

Make sure that those closest to you ...

> *are chosen intentionally!*
> *are connected to your core values!*
> *are compelled by things that are noble and pure!*
> *are called to be there, and you know why they have come!*

are concerned about your spiritual health more than anything else!
are committed to bring out the best in you!

Sound Investing

Investing in relational connections ...

always a good idea ... always!
awakens realities that need to be activated!
missing this means you lose big!
always adds and never takes away!
guarantees that you will get rich payback!
takes time but not energy!

Be Diligent about Friendships

Be diligent to nurture friendships because ...

they will bless you for a lifetime!
they are a worthwhile investment!
everything you give will be given back to you!
relational connections matter!
you can never replace them!
each one is a special, unique gift!
being rich in friends is a very good thing!

Be a Quality Person

Seek to be the kind of person that ...

others can depend on, no matter what!
solves problems for others, not creates them!
adds value to others, not takes away!
others want to tune in to, not tune out!

can confront what needs to be confronted, and yet still be kind to others!
others want to be around, not avoid!
makes others feel safe, not on the edge!

Passion is Contagious!

Spending time with passionate people ...

makes it impossible to stay where you are!
makes the powerful impact of passion obvious!
will inspire you to give your heart away!
makes it clear that passion poured out is explosive!
makes you believe that they really can change the world!
will redefine "enthusiasm" for you!

Strengthen Your Friendships

Friendships are strengthened by ...

spending time together ... doing anything!
special moments ... celebrated together!
showing up and being there ... just because!
saying all that needs to be said ... in the moment that it needs to be spoken!
stepping into every situation ... no matter what it takes!
sharing ordinary moments ... over and over again!
staying close ... in good times and bad!

Proactively Bless Others

Since we can never know what is happening in the lives of those we interact with ...

share a blessing!
promote the good!
listen, then speak!

offer to help!
assume the best!
always be attentive!
show you care!

Pursue the "New" with Others

Enjoying new experiences, making new memories and finding new friends ...

be intentional in making this happen!
always an option to consider!
you gotta keep adding to life!
this is as good as it gets!
you will never grow old if you do this!
can be a little risky!
these are the things that make life special!

Revive Old Connections

Reconnecting with an old friend ...

seems to make time stand still!
makes you aware of just how much things have changed after all!
there is an awareness that what "was" still "is"!
amazing to be reminded of just how much you have forgotten!
makes you appreciate just how special lifelong friendships really are!
there is no way to measure the depth of how great that feels!
awakens yesterday in your heart!

The Blessing Is in the Doing

Here is something you can do for others that is always appreciated ...

pray for them purposefully!
touch them tenderly!
offer them hospitality!
respond to them graciously!
love them lavishly!
encourage them openly!

A Better Life

Life is always better ...

when you lift people up!
when you show people that you believe in them!
when you give people the best of you!
when you surprise people with kindness!
when you love people with your heart wide open!

Time = Love

Spending time with special friends ...

simply adds increased value to what you already treasure!
a guaranteed "yes" for me!
now that can be addictive!
no additional set-up needed!
always works no matter who they are or where you meet!
you never run out of things to say!
is always a valuable investment!

The Right People Make All the Difference!

You know you are hanging with the right people ...

when you keep getting together, over and over again!

when the stories and memories you share never end!

when you both look for ways to create a win-win in every situation!

you know they will give you the automatic "Yes"!

when every time they call, you want to answer!

when they can see the best in the worst of you!

Be Open to New Relationships

Meeting a lot of new people at the moment ...

and nothing is better for me than that!

and I just marvel at the circumstances that bring us together!

and every one is special in their own way!

and I am taken by the timing of it all!

and it is amazing how quickly you can connect!

and I am one happy guy!

Simply Meet Desperate Needs

Things others most desperately need are the simplest gifts for us to give ...

a loyal friendship!

a shoulder to cry on!

a word of blessing!

a sense of value!

a reason to smile!

a warm embrace!

an extravagant grace!

Appreciate Great Friendships

You know that you have a great friend when ...

> *your shared history is deeper than you ever imagined possible!*
>
> *apologies are not necessary, but when offered they are immediately accepted!*
>
> *they dare to confront you!*
>
> *you can tell them everything knowing that they won't share anything!*
>
> *they know the worst about you and yet still believe the best!*
>
> *they try to find a soft way to tell you what you seriously need to hear!*
>
> *simple moments become spectacular!*

Quality Friends are Beneficial

Great friends ...

> *always give more than they take!*
>
> *last a lifetime!*
>
> *you cannot do life without them!*
>
> *just thinking about them always brings a smile!*
>
> *always celebrate with you on your good days and carry you on the bad ones!*
>
> *never give up or go away!*
>
> *the best gift you can give yourself!*

Share Your Life

Sharing life, showing love and staying strong ...

find a way ... to make these things happen!

finally ... these are simply powerful life priorities!

failure ... a real possibility, so never let up!

first steps ... that lead to a certain final destination!

fabulous way to live ... every day, all day!

full-time job ... do remember that!

Life Reflection

Jesus said, "Therefore, if you are offering your gift at the altar and there remember that your brother has something against you, leave your gift there in front of the altar. First go and be reconciled to your brother; then come and offer your gift" (Matthew 5:23-24). This is an amazing statement which reveals to us the value that God places on human relationships.

◊ *Jesus' teaching in Matthew 5 seems to say, that in God's mind, our relationship with Him (vertical) seems to be deeply woven with our relationships with others (horizontal). The two relational dimensions cannot be separated. Does this surprise you? Are there any implications for you with your current state of relationships?*

◊ *Reflect on your primary family of origin. It's in this setting, during the early years of our development, that we begin to learn about relationships. Without dishonoring our family of origin, remember that Jesus redefined our most intimate relationships ... "'Who is my mother, and who are my brothers?' Pointing to his disciples, he said, 'Here are my mother and my brothers. For whoever does the will of my Father in heaven is my brother and sister and mother'" (Matthew 12:48-50). In what ways is Jesus transforming you as you relate to others? He wants to bring you to a new level.*

◊ *Think of 3 relationships which can be strengthened in your life. What are the first 3 that quickly come to mind? Now, having read this chapter, what is one thing you can do right away to enhance each of those relationships?*

Prayer & Affirmation

Father, I take comfort in your heart, for you are a God of deep relationship. Thank you for who you are. And because I am created in your image, I too am a person with deep relational capacity.

Jesus Christ has broken down walls and reconciled all things to you, Father. I am a new creation in Christ. You have committed to me the ministry of reconciliation. I am an ambassador for Christ (2 Corinthians 5:17-20).

Though I live in a fallen world of estranged relationships, I will be different. I will courageously pursue healthy relationships. I will model for others what is possible.

Father, continue to work deeply within my heart. "See if there is any offensive way in me, and lead me in the way everlasting" (Psalm 139:24). I give you glory because you are healing and restoring me. I will live whole-heartedly.

Enhance every relationship in my life. Bring new connections to my life in harmony with your design. I know that the energy of your Kingdom flows through these connections.

May you be glorified in all things. May something of your fame be known through my relational life.

Amen.

ABOUND IN

"People who promote hope ... put apathy on alert!"
— Terry

Here's a powerful force-multiplier in your life!

Let's remember this: without hope, we cannot have faith ... *"Now faith is being sure of what we hope for and certain of what we do not see" (Hebrews 11:1).*

Here's some good news. Not only does faith come from God, hope comes from Him ... *"May the God of hope fill you with all joy and peace as you trust in him, so that you may overflow with hope by the power of the Holy Spirit" (Romans 15:13).*

But we have to be intentional about hope. We must passionately desire to be a hope-overflowing person in this world. And of course, all of this

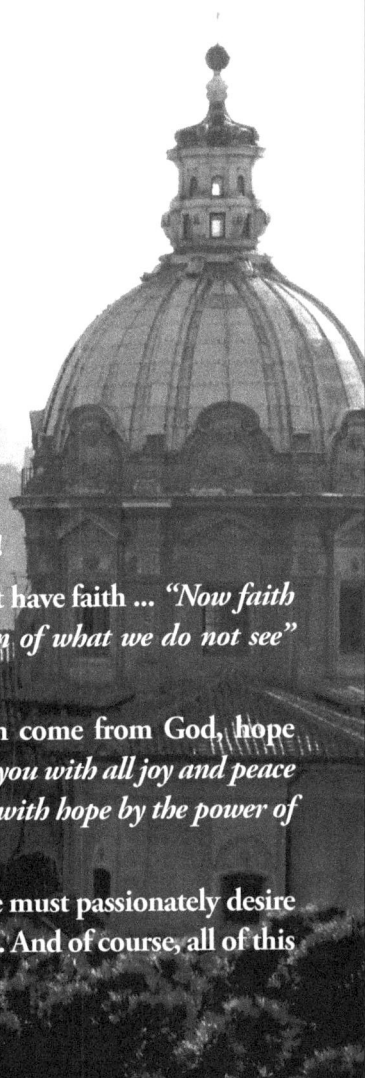

is sourced in our trust in God Almighty, as we walk in step with His Spirit.

Scripturally, to wait upon the Lord means *to lean forward with a hopeful expectation of good.* We are anticipating the very expression of God's nature in our lives.

> *"Those who hope (or wait) on the Lord will renew their strength. They will soar on wings like eagles; they will run and not grow weary, they will walk and not be faint" (Isaiah 40:31).*

So are you ready for more hope? Are you weary of hopelessness? An unlimited amount of hope is available. Let's go for it!

Allow Hope to Overflow

When your heart is full of hope ...

> *you want to give it away!*
>
> *your spirit will soar and your heart will be strong!*
>
> *you'll make being a "hope-giver" your priority!*
>
> *you'll pray for hope to come, promote hope and personally ask the God of all hope to help us!*
>
> *the future is full of promise!*
>
> *you can see possibilities in every problem!*
>
> *there will be a feeling of deep, deep joy!*
>
> *believing for something new is easy!*
>
> *you can overcome anything!*

Advance Hope

People who promote hope ...

> *make our world a better place!*
>
> *live to give!*
>
> *push life!*
>
> *know the power of hope ... personally!*

put apathy on alert!
choose to be one!

Walking in Hope

Walking thru a tough time ...

keep walking ... it is not going to last forever!
refines and defines us!
only a great friend will be with you there!
will make us better if we do not get bitter!
is no place for the "why" question ... we have to think "how" or "what"!
tests the best of us!
always know that you will never walk alone!

Chase the Blues Away with Hope

There are lots of great ways to chase the blues away ...

like believing that it won't rain always! The sun will shine again!
like savoring the reality that you are special to God!
like reflecting on all the ways you have loved and have been loved!
like embracing God's promise to bless you, give you hope and a future!
like showing compassion to someone in need!
like taking a moment to celebrate those who actually deserve to be celebrated!
like doing something completely silly that makes you laugh!

Expect!

The wonderful thing about hopeful expectation is ...

it gives you life!
you always have something to look forward to!
you begin believing!

it promotes a deep longing in your heart!
it nurtures a positive perspective!

Hope Overcomes

take on the challenge and enjoy the thrill!
stay focused on your dream and keep dreaming still!
battle on and battle until!
laugh out loud and laugh until!
hold your head high and be confident still!
keep on walking and walk until!

How Is Your Sight?

The thing about perspective is that ...

what it produces provides all the evidence you need to know to determine what kind of perspective you have!
it regulates your response!
it decides whose voice matters!
it can be influenced by everything!
only you can decide to change it!
it impacts your attitude!
it colors how you see your world!

Perspective Makes the Difference

Perspective is more than a point of view ...

it makes us or breaks us!
it decides what kind of person I will be!
it colors my word in every way!
it determines our response!
it defines our focus!

it sets the rhythm of life for us!
it shapes our attitude!

Even in Pain There Is Hope

It is tough for me when ...

I see hope dying!
I see intentional prejudice!
I see the needy ignored!
I see the fragile violated!
I see relationships broken!
I see people hurting!

See the Past Through the Lens of Hope

The only way to deal with your past in a positive way is to ...

not let anything hold you captive there!
keep it behind you!
be healed of any pain and celebrate your freedom!
not allow it to take anything from you!
remember the good and recall it often!
take the lessons learned with you!
only take a glance when looking back, but gaze into your future!

The Good Is There ... Look for It

Being able to see the good ...

is a gift to you and to others!
is in deciding that it has to be intentional!
is in recognizing that it is your call!
is in developing a positive, faith perspective!
is in accepting that it is a challenge that needs to be conquered!

is in knowing that confirming the good is more helpful that criticizing the bad!

is in believing that it is there to be found!

are caring, loving, healthy people ... it does matter!

Lean Forward with Hope

Living forward ...

> *it is our call!*
>
> *allows us to walk into our tomorrows!*
>
> *anything else robs and ruins!*
>
> *puts hope at the front of our hearts!*
>
> *this is the healthy, honorable way to live!*

Life Reflection

So, what is the level of your "hope meter?" Are you overflowing with hope? Half-filled? Empty? God wants you to overflow with hope in the Spirit's power. Is this a new perspective for you?

◊ *Our faith-level is directly correlated to our hope-level. See Hebrews 11:1 again. Quite often, it's helpful to think in terms of process in our spiritual development. So, if we feel we need faith for something, we probably want to start with building our hope in the promises of the Word, targeting that concern. Will you invest the time to fuel your hope and faith with the Word?*

◊ *By the way, faith (and faith's precursor, hope) comes to us by hearing the living voice of the Lord via the written Word, and the voice of His Spirit to us! What will you do to fine-tune your ears of faith?*

◊ *Reflect on this question ... are you leaning forward into your future with a hopeful expectation of good from the Lord? His essential nature is good! And His plans for you are to give you His ideas about your hope-designed future (see Jeremiah 29:11-13).*

Prayer & Affirmation

Father, I freely acknowledge ... you are the God of all hope! Your passion is to fill me with hope until I overflow on everyone and everything around me.

I resolve afresh to listen attentively to your living voice via your Word, and via the voice of your Spirit to me. There is so much noise around me. There is even noise within me! Help me to hear the signal of your signature voice through all the noise. Let it become my dominant life-sound!

I lean into today, this week, this month, this year with a hopeful expectation of good from You! I renounce the Adversary's lies about who you are. You are goodness! And your plans for me are to lift the shades and open the windows to a wonderful future! Let me feel the fresh breezes of your Spirit. I'm grateful.

Give me new levels of discernment, a greater clarity. Help me, Holy Spirit, to see and comprehend my real future.

Thank you, Father, for everything. I am a person of extraordinary hope. I count it done in Jesus' name.

SEE AND PURSUE THE
OPPORTUNITY

"Dynamic opportunities ... are always present but must be passionately pursued!"
— Terry

I don't need to tell you that we live in a fallen world. The effects of humanity's disobedience are all around us. We feel it every week! Even so, amazingly, opportunities abound! Especially for the Christ-follower.

Many times, we live as if our potential is directly correlated to our own natural means ... personal history, heredity, financial resources, education, relational network, and so on.

The reality is we should live as if our personal world has no ceiling.

When Mary asked the angel, *"How can this be?"*, heaven's response was that the Holy Spirit would overshadow her. *"With God, all things are possible."* What it literally says in the native language of the New

Testament is, *"There is not one word of God which is devoid of power to fulfill the promise spoken."*

As Mary, we can live in alignment with the resources of heaven! We can harmonize our lives with the expressed thoughts of God to us.

But we'll have to put away negativity and unbelief. For the Christ-follower, those are aspects of our old nature. Here's the ultimate opportunity(!) — you can now seek to consistently live in agreement with your new nature in Christ.

Tap the Dynamism of Opportunity!

Dynamic opportunities ...

> *blessed is the person who sees and seeks them!*
> *are often surrounded by difficult obstacles!*
> *are more the result of how we choose to live, not our luck!*
> *can be difficult to release but are still within our reach!*
> *are developed and discerned, not simply discovered!*
> *rarely just come your way, they are strategically sought out!*
> *are always present but must be passionately pursued!*

Opportunity in the Unexpected

Expect the unexpected ...

> *it always happens ... so be ready for it!*
> *and keep your mind focused and your heart at peace!*
> *it makes all the difference in the world!*
> *it will make you better at so many levels!*
> *and never lose that discipline!*
> *and save yourself a lot of wasted time and energy!*
> *and live not being surprised!*

The Opportunity Is in the Learning

Always learning and being willing to be taught ...

this is how I want to live!
challenges you to stay connected!
consider the alternative ... scary huh!
guarantees that you will always have something to give!
sharpens your skill!
assures that you will stay relevant!
a necessary leadership reality!

Live with Honor and Faith

Walking with honor and living by faith ...

pulls you up and does the same for others!
places you among quality people!
positions you to succeed!
provides hope and blessing!
protects you from shame and disappointment!
promotes an abundance of opportunity!

Be Real About Opportunity

The truth about opportunity ...

it is always risky to embrace, so don't be afraid of it!
it is always available but costly to access, so be ready to pay for it!
it is always open for debate to those who doubt it, so just believe in it!
it is often disguised, so dig for it!
it is always present, so expect to find it!
it is rare and filled with potential, so don't miss it!

Take on that Challenge!

Here is the truth about a challenge ...

pushing thru is the best thing to do!

making a plan will help you to stand!

taking it on makes you strong!

believing that you can overcome assures that it cannot!

hoping that it will go away only guarantees that it is here to stay!

getting over it is easier than getting around it!

facing it is better than fearing it!

Opportunity Necessitates Transition

Most of life's transitions are ...

undeniably significant ... they shape our destiny!

undervalued ... they truly change us more than they challenge us!

unnerving, so we need to be ready to engage and not be emotional!

unexpected, so we need real stability to deal with radical surprises!

unplanned so somehow we have to live ready to respond correctly and accurately!

Embrace New Experiences

Enjoying new experiences, making new memories and finding new friends ...

be intentional in making this happen!

always an option to consider!

you gotta keep adding to life!

this is as good as it gets!

you will never grow old if you do this!

can be a little risky!

these are the things that make life special!

New Initiatives are Your Friends

This seems to be a special moment for new initiatives and opportunities ...

don't let anyone steal your dream!
all things are possible you know!
destiny is written in all of our hearts!
time to live engaging and expecting!
there is no doubt that the best thing is the next thing!
seeing dynamic movement is amazing!
very exciting to see dreams fulfilled!

The Benefits of a Challenge

What's the point of taking on a challenge ...

it proves that you are taking on life!
it provides you with opportunity!
it confirms your tenacity!
it demonstrates your skill!
it expands your comfort zone!
it defines your capacity!
it pushes the extremes of your potential!

Opportunity Is Often Hidden in Difficulty

When we can see opportunity in every obstacle ...

we will be better people in so many ways!
we will make those around us better!
we will bring life to whatever we do!
we will live more fulfilled and less frustrated!
we will become much more creative!
we will lose our "excuse-making" skill!
we will accomplish more!

Go for Your Personal Best!

If you intend to achieve your best ...

>*think like a winner!*
>
>*pay the price!*
>
>*get outside your comfort zone!*
>
>*quit making excuses!*
>
>*aim high and do not settle for less!*
>
>*make the tough decisions!*
>
>*activate your dream!*

Turn to What's New

Doing something new is a good thing because ...

>*we want to become all that we are intended to be!*
>
>*we are a work in progress!*
>
>*only when life is fully engaged is it fully enjoyed!*
>
>*being bored is bad news!*
>
>*in reaching for more we release our potential!*
>
>*it makes life richer!*
>
>*we have to move beyond our well-established routines and limitations!*

Life Reflection

In the face of living in a fallen, broken world, there is much opportunity. Much more than we realize! Especially as we seek God and follow Christ with renewed passion. And that's just it — we have to face brokenness with faith!

Here's a positive affirmation for your life ... there is no ceiling for you! Not when you're with God. "Nothing will be impossible with God" (Luke 1:37 NASB). The NIV gives us the sense of the original words to Mary: "For no word from God will ever fail." This is where the hope comes from—what is God saying to you?

◊ *Have you been trying to live as if your potential is directly correlated to your own natural means?*

◊ *What has God spoken into your life? Do you need to excavate any of those words from deep within your heart? What may He be speaking to you now?*

◊ *Are you motivated about living in alignment with the resources of heaven! Can you see yourself rising higher?*

Prayer & Affirmation

Father, I say that "nothing is impossible with you." And I'm with you, so there is no ceiling over my head. I am head over all things.

I'm blessed with every spiritual blessing in the heavenlies in Christ (Ephesians 1:3). Teach me, Holy Spirit, how to live in alignment with heaven's resources for me, and for my family and domain. I'm ready to learn fresh, new things.

My potential is not tethered to natural means. I press toward the mark of the high calling of God in Christ. I will seize that destiny for which Christ Jesus laid hold of me. I repent—turning from the past—and reaching forward to what's ahead. I will live by this new standard I'm attaining in Christ. (See Philippians 3:12-16.)

My potential is resourced by supernatural means! Thank you, Father, for making me rise higher and higher.

So, I renounce the old pre-Christ nature, and I now live in harmony with my new nature in Christ. I say with Mary, "Amen—let it be to me as you have spoken."

THE FORCE OF A

QUALITY DECISION

*"Make decisions that ... reflect your values
and reveal your passion!"*
— Terry

God honors our decisions.

What do you desire? What is your intent?

Jesus asked sick people, *"What do you want?"* and *"Do you want to be
well?"* This is pretty amazing. We must have desire. And we must express
that desire through quality decision-making.

If you make a decision to draw near to God, then He will draw near to
you (James 4:8). See how heaven responds to our initiative?

Heaven and earth are watching what we will choose.

> *"This day I call heaven and earth as witnesses against you that I have
> set before you life and death, blessings and curses. Now choose life, so*

that you and your children may live and that you may love the Lord your God, listen to his voice, and hold fast to him." (Deuteronomy 30:19-20)

Not only is heaven watching. The earth is watching ... circumstances and natural phenomena will respond, eventually aligning to our strong intent.

What do we need to make great decisions? We need the best information—and Jesus has the best information for us. And we need the confidence to step up and step forward as we trust our Lord with the decisions we make. Heaven and earth are waiting.

The Significance of the First Time
Getting things right the first time matters because ...

> *you never get a second chance to make a first impression!*
> *it guarantees rapid development and growth!*
> *it reveals that your assessments are accurate!*
> *it assures that your inclusion plan works!*
> *it proves that your team efficiencies are being maximized!*
> *it confirms that your decision-making process is effective!*
> *it eliminates frustration and failure!*

The Benefit of Deeper Thinking
When you need to think thru something ...

> *do what is best and nothing less!*
> *it is always best to take the time you need to see ... what you need to see!*
> *it is always best to test your conclusions to assure that they are accurate!*
> *it is always best to confirm that the context is correct ... so be certain!*
> *it is always best to make it a well-documented process ... keep a journal!*
> *it is always best to think with someone ... a trusted, wise someone!*

Making a Difference by Choice

Choosing to live making a difference ...

is the only thing to make life worth living!

assures that we will live for things that really matter!

does not require a lot from us ... it requires everything!

means that we will have increasing influence and impact!

is not really a noble act ... it is a necessary one!

Get Strategic!

The thing about strategic planning ...

is that in aiming at something we will achieve more!

is that we will be more attentive and expectant!

is that we can tend to minimize today by looking beyond it ... but today matters!

is that by engaging we are well-prepared for embracing!

is that we are intentionally preparing for a positive outcome ... somehow!

is that we risk assuming too much ... so keep it real!

is that living with a long-term vision is much better than living with a short-term view!

Passion Will Not Be Denied

Passionate pursuit is powerful ...

so stay on mission!

so see your pathway clearly and carry on!

so step up and embrace your dream!

so set every distraction aside!

so settle in your heart and mind what you want to go after!

so strengthen your resolve to push on!

so seek what calls to your heart!

Be Proactive with Your Response

Words, actions, responses and reactions ...

these are the things that do matter ... believe that!

these are the things that develop the pathway that we will take ... believe that!

these are the things that decide how people see us ... believe that!

these are the things that declare the deepest part of who we are ... believe that!

these are the things that determine whether we will live large or be small ... believe that!

these are the things that drive us ... believe that!

these are the things that define us ... believe that!

Desire Deeply

My desire is to live a passion-driven, purpose-focused, principle-centered life

and that seriously works for me!

so I intentionally evaluate everything!

so staying on mission matters!

and I am working at it every day!

so I always have a plan!

so I intentionally have a clear set of priorities!

and I love where that takes me!

We Can Choose

When given the chance to choose ...

choose to make amends!

choose to hold on!

choose to go for it!

choose to do more!
choose to act first!
choose to be there!

Passion is Contagious

I love being around passionate people ...

their energy is life-giving!
their plans are stunning!
their concepts are outrageous!
their focus is intense!
their ideas are incredible!
their conversations are provoking!

Daily Decisions

Every day you have to decide ...

what will you do to fulfill your destiny? And not deciding, is a decision!
what will you be a part of? And not deciding, is a decision!
what will you take on? And not deciding, is a decision!
what will you let go of? And not deciding, is a decision!
what will you live for? And not deciding, is a decision!
what will you do to make a difference? And not deciding, is a decision!
what will you do and who will you become? And not deciding, is a decision!

Be Confident In Your Decision-Making

Make decisions that ...

need to be made ... with no delay!
prove that you are thinking, telling the truth and taking a stand!
are just and fair not biased and judgemental!

reflect your values and reveal your passion!
you do not have to apologize for!
are based on the right input, not risky impulse!
set you up for success!

Decisive People Make an Impact!

I love decisive people ...

they keep leaders sharp!
they are always motivated to move things along and make things happen!
they will not waste time, effort or energy ... for any issue, reason or person!
they process quickly, put things in order and produce action!
they see it, say it and settle it!
they want to be measured by what they do ... not by what they talk about doing!
they keep meetings short!

Good Leadership Creates Movement

Great leaders always find a way to ...

respond rapidly!
talk team!
encourage expectancy!
constructively confront!
accelerate action!

Life Reflection

Are you comfortable with the understanding that Jesus is interested in what we desire? And that heaven honors our decisions?

◊   *What do you desire right now? What do you want? What's the very first one, two, or three things that surface in your heart? Don't over-think it, simply let your heart answer. Your heart-answer will feel like it comes from a deep place instead of the surface of your mind.*

◊   *Are you decisive? Or, do you struggle with double mindedness? Consider that an insincere mind will neutralize what we are able to receive from God … "But when you ask, you must believe and not doubt, because the one who doubts is like a wave of the sea, blown and tossed by the wind. That person should not expect to receive anything from the Lord. Such a person is double-minded and unstable in all they do" (James 1:6-8).*

◊   *Heaven and earth are watching your life. Does this cause you to fear, or does it motivate you?*

◊   *Do you need better information from Jesus? For what?*

Prayer & Affirmation

Jesus, I know you are keenly interested in what I desire. And I know you perfectly represent the Father's heart. So, Father, I praise you for having my interests at heart. Truly, you are a Father of the heart.

Holy Spirit, assist me in articulating my heart accurately before the Father. I receive your illumination ... your expressed thoughts. Father, I come boldly before your throne of grace.

Father, help me to be heart-oriented. Teach me how to live from my heart. More and more, I want my heart to resonate with yours. I want to take delight in you, and experience my heart's desires. I commit my ways to you in trust. You will do it all through me. See Psalm 37:4-5.

I have the mind of Christ. I have access to the best information in the universe. I am decisive. So, I request from a place of strong resolution before the King of kings.

I like it that heaven and earth are watching me. I enjoy it. Father, may my life be a theatre of who you are, and of what you intend to do.

Amen.

LIVING ON A
HIGHER PLANE

When we're born again through belief in Jesus Christ, we're not just going to heaven someday. We're newly designed to live on a higher plane with Christ now! We're called to give witness to the higher quality of life that God offers ... eternal life.

God calls us to the heights— *"The Sovereign LORD is my strength; he makes my feet like the feet of a deer, he enables me to tread on the heights" (Habakkuk 3:19).* Each of us has personal heights for which we are designed.

Even more ... we are also commissioned to possess the heights of our enemies— *"Blessed are you, Israel! Who is like you, a people saved by the LORD? He is your shield and helper and your glorious sword. Your enemies will cower before you, and you will tread on their heights" (Deuteronomy 33:29).*

The Christ-follower has a new nature. As we learn to live from our new nature and not the old, we progressively learn how to live from a higher plane. This is where Christianity gets exciting!

Consider the thoughts on the next several pages. Pray them. Put them in the first person singular and use them as personal affirmations. As you do, I believe you will condition your inner man so that you can live from a higher plane.

Offer Thanks

Everyone needs to take a moment to say thanks ...

> *for all the hope that has sustained us!*
> *for all the things that have blessed us!*
> *for all the love that has found us!*
> *for all the good that we have been given!*
> *for all the kindness that we have been shown!*

Clear and Convincing Communication

Being able to communicate with clarity and conviction ...

> *gives you an edge in almost everything, so work on this at all costs!*
> *enables your message to have greater potential to provoke a response!*
> *guarantees that you will always get your point across!*
> *when you see people who have it, you know it instantly!*
> *may not be automatic for you but it can be acquired!*
> *assures that you better learn to like being a spokesperson!*
> *may be a gift ... but treat it like an art!*

Get Ready for Surprises

When surprises come, and they surely will ...

remember that your future is secure even still!
do the best you can and leave the rest in His hands!
it is your focus that will keep you moving uphill!
be ready to adjust, that is always a must!
stay your course and strengthen your will!
be quick to respond because there is no magic wand!
take them on knowing that they are part of life's thrill!

Pursue Health

If you want to stay healthy in every way ...

keep dreaming ... and don't let anyone steal your dreams!
stay inside the boundaries ... where God's love dominates!
avoid exaggerations and extremes ... in everything!
lose the tyranny of anger ... find a way to let it go!
stop making excuses ... just take care of business!
keep forgiving yourself ... and others!
celebrate what others achieve ... don't criticize or compare!

Great Feelings

One of the greatest feelings in the world ...

is always found when we give and go beyond ourselves!
is being surprised by good!
is hope restored when everything seemed lost!
is when you can make a wrong ... right!
is seeing the dawn while still walking in the dark!

is when a challenging project is completed!
is making someone else's dream come true!

Be That Person

Be the kind of person ...

who can put everything right ... in a moment!
who can wisely intervene and get results!
who can positively step in and make a difference ... always!
who can push back and still be respected!
who can politely say what needs to be said ... and then stop!
who can purposefully interrupt and be interrupted!
who can patiently handle the worst and still believe the best!

Grateful People are Great People

Really grateful people ...

will find the smallest patch of blue sky!
bring a lift to any crowd or circumstance!
can seriously do Thanksgiving Day!
tend to be much more positive people!
are amazing at celebrating the little things!
see favor, know goodness and desire blessing!

It's the Right Thing

It is only right ...

to be sacrificial in serving!
to give more than you take!
to be faithful in forgiving!
to heal and not hate!
to bless and not break!

to live generously!
to love extravagantly!

Be Extraordinary

In order to be your best ...

keep reaching!
push beyond "acceptable"!
be determined to make daily, measurable progress!
actually change and not just talk about it!
freely admit that you are not there yet!
accept constructive criticism without being defensive!
be honest about where you are!

Keep Seeking

I really wish I knew ...

more ways to show love to others!
how to end a nasty conversation graciously but honestly!
what to say in every situation!
an easy fix for a broken relationship!
the best solution for bringing calm in chaos!
all the answers to life's toughest questions!
the way to touch people who seem untouchable!

Better to Best!

Things we can all do better ...

solve more problems than we create!
think twice before we do or say anything!
confront ourselves before we start on others!
live by what we know not by what we feel!

give more support and less advice!
lose the excuses so real change can happen!
be intentionally kind and seek the good!

How then Should We Live?

We do have a higher call ... but what are we doing about it?
Here is how you want to live ...

engaged but not always exhausted!
disappointed but not always discouraged!
believing the best but not always seeing!
making a difference but not always knowing!
battling but not always broken!
thinking but not always talking!
loving but not always understanding!

Life Is Full of Beauty

The beauty of life ...

is always present but often unseen ... so be one who sees!
is being able to see yourself and others from a positive perspective!
is in being generous in giving and gracious in receiving!
is in seeing opportunity in every obstacle!
is something we create as a gift to ourselves!
is in capturing the small moments and celebrating the big ones!
is really seen in things most often taken for granted!

Never Again!

Things that I can never do again ...

> *let busyness dictate my time and my heart!*
>
> *stand by quietly!*
>
> *accept that any coffee or cappuccino made with a powder is real!*
>
> *ignore my health!*
>
> *believe the media!*
>
> *eat french fries without mayonnaise!*

Life Reflection

As a disciple of Christ, you are recreated to live from a higher place. Paul wrote that "God raised us up with Christ and seated us with him in the heavenly realms in Christ Jesus" (Ephesians 2:6). Now we have to practically learn how to lead our lives from this place of privilege.

◊   *Have you ever thought that our testimony of Christ and his kingdom is more than words? It is also the quality of life we live. As others watch our lives, do they sense that we're living from a higher place?*

◊   *As far as you can see now, what are those personal heights you feel called to possess? What about the heights of the Adversary?*

◊   *What are those things (think of several) which cause you to be more connected with your new nature? Maybe it's something like meditation. Major on those things.*

◊   *And what are those things which cause you to be more connected with your lower, older nature? Ruthlessly seek to eliminate those things.*

Prayer & Affirmation

Heavenly Father, I praise you for lifting me out of the mire and seating me with Christ in heavenly places.

Now show me how to live from that place back "down" into earth-born situations. I'm not down here trying to live "upward." I'm with Christ, living from a superior place of privilege and responsibility.

I thank you that your glory has risen upon me. Darkness may be covering everything and everyone, but the Lord has risen upon me and his glory appears over me. May the people come to my light and kings to the brightness of my dawn. See Isaiah 60:1-3.

Father cause me to possess the heights you've called me to. I commit to it.

I resolve afresh to live from my new nature and not the old. I will sacrifice anything to do this. No cost is too high. It's that important to me.

The dominion is yours, King Jesus.

Amen.

CELEBRATE

"The beauty of life ... is in capturing the small moments and celebrating the big ones!"
— Terry

Life is meant to be celebrated!

If our view of God is dour and sour—and then the "Christian" life we live is the same—we have an incomplete or inaccurate view of God.

Think of it. God established that the Israelites were to celebrate seven times each year at the Jewish feasts. All of the men were commanded to travel to Jerusalem for three of those feasts each year. The Scriptures teach that we are to come into the presence of God with thanksgiving and joy.

Jesus tells us that He came to give us life. And life more abundantly! (John 10:10). Are you leaning into the "more" of Christ's life?

Do you feel chronically weak? There could be a number of reasons including eating habits, quality of sleep, and our discipline of exercise. But one of the issues we should explore is our joy level— *"Go and enjoy choice food and sweet drinks, and send some to those who have nothing prepared. This day is holy to our Lord. Do not grieve, for the joy of the LORD is your strength"* (Nehemiah 8:10).

Do you see that? AUTHENTIC JOY = STRENGTH.

Embrace Autumn

Fall has come and it's time to ...

celebrate another great reason for living in Brussels ... beautiful here!

put those sweaters on!

make plans for a hayride!

enjoy a great cup of coffee all the more!

take in a high school football game!

get the soup on!

slow down and appreciate the beauty of it all!

Advent ... the Coming

The season of Advent has just started ...

so use these days to make this Christmas extra-special!

share the joy of giving!

speak life and show love!

set the right priorities!

seek to reflect the spirit of the Christ!

start now to get your heart ready!

so do all you can to make these days count!

Anticipating Christmas

The Christmas countdown begins ...

and it just gets better and better!

Christmastime is here!

humming, whistling and singing all my favorite Christmas carols ... all the time!

celebrate something Christmassy every day!

so be less naughty and more nice!

time to share the love!

I know what I want to do ... do you?

make the most of these days of Christmas!

Don't just count down the days of Christmas ...

live them ... they are way too special to waste!

redeem them ... each one offers unique opportunities!

prioritize them ... and make each one precious!

embrace them ... they are always full of potential!

capture the spirit of Christmas ... and share it with everyone!

make the most of them ... in every way!

celebrate them ... big time!

Christmas Week

This is Christmas week ...

a great time to remember that wise men still seek!

and now we know ... everything is possible when we let His love show!

and though Christmas Day has passed, let's do all we can to make the spirit last!

a great time to remember that those who win are the meek!

a great time to remember that Christ deserves more than a peek!

so I want to say, "May the presence of Christ and the promise of Christmas be yours in every way!"

Christmas Infuses Hope!

Christmas reminds us that hope has come ...

so make sure everyone knows!
and life is renewed!
and hope gives birth to great things!
and that changes everything!
and when hope is present, dreams live!
and that may well be the best gift of all!
and we need hope now more than ever before!

The Highest Gifts

The greatest gifts of Christmas are the ones that cannot be bought and do not need bows ...

like finding a passion that never grows cold!
like building a faith that will not fold!
like having a friendship that cannot be bought ... or sold!
like saying positive things to each other that need to be told!
like making memories that you can treasure and hold!
like sharing a love that is big and bold!
like spending time together ... that never grows old!

A New Year Is a Fresh Start

Let's make the new year a really great year by being attentive to …

the kind of prayers that we pray!
the decisions that we take!
the things that we choose to lose!

the company that we keep!
the focus that we seek!
the plans that you make!
the path that you choose!

Look for 'the New' in a New Year!

New Year's Eve—a time of celebration, reflection and expectation! I will make every effort to end well and begin right!

A fresh year will bring many things ...

celebrate all that is good, change all that is bad and let God take care of all the rest!

over which we have control, but we do have choices! My heart aches for the innocent in the Paris attacks ... and for the guilty!

nothing will stay the same ... so we cannot either!

all of which will either need to be enjoyed, embraced or eliminated!

so now is the time to make ourselves ready!

none of which have the power to break us or bless us. We will decide that all by ourselves!

too much potential to push aside!

Step Over the Threshold

The dawning of the new year is a threshold moment ...

too significant to squander!
too good to goof up!
begin it the way you want to end it!
wrap up the old year right!
too important to ignore!
too wonderful to waste!

Valentine's Day

Valentine's Day this week ...

so let the love flow ... honestly everything will be better!

so make sure that those you love feel extra-special ... this will call for intentional activity!

so this should be a special week for everyone! Do your part!

so find a way to share loving support! So many options to consider!

so be extra-kind ... all week long!

so make the most of every opportunity to say, "I love you!" ... it is worth it!

Spring Renews

When Spring finally gets here ...

I think I will do an American, Italian and Swedish style picnic ... long overdue!

I think I may just whistle every day!

I am seriously going to take so many photos!

I will be inventing new adjectives to describe it!

I am going to do my happy dance!

Easter reminds us that ...

joyful expectation will be greatly rewarded!

new things are promised!

dark days will not last!

impossible possibilities do exist!

real change can happen!

living hope is an option!

Happy Birthday!

Just had my birthday and here is what I learned ...

the most important birthday of all ... is this one!

every age has its advantages ... and disadvantages!

the greatest memories come from the smallest things ... so take time for the small things!

I have the greatest friends ever ... and so do you!

seeing the "then" and "now" photos will make you "philosophical ... and depressed!"

being celebrated by others is a great morale boost ... so celebrate everyone!

Getting older guarantees that ...

faith, family and friends will greatly increase in value!

you will experience a paradigm shift!

the desire to finish well becomes fervent determination!

more things will hurt than ever before!

embracing a new reality is an inescapable fact!

even you can't believe that it is you in the old photos that you see!

Life Reflection

What is your CQ ... your Celebration Quotient? If 3 people who know you well were to rate how well you celebrate life, what would they say?

◊ *Is there anything in your background or life experience which would cause you to be challenged with this statement: GOD IS JOY PERSONIFIED?*

◊ *How intensely are you leaning into the fullness of Christ's quality of life? "The thief comes only to steal and kill and destroy; I have come that they may have life, and have it to the full" (John 10:10).*

◊ *Do you think there are those times or seasons where you have to contend to celebrate life? If so, how are you doing with that?*

◊ *If Satan comes to "steal and kill and destroy," could celebrating the life of Jesus in a moment by moment way be considered an expression of spiritual warfare? Are you willing to fight for it?*

◊ *If you were to rate the CQ of your 5 closest relationships, what would the average be? Would it bother you if I said that your CQ is most likely close to the average CQ of these relationships?*

Prayer & Affirmation

Father, I understand that you are a God of joy. You value celebration.

Heal me of anything in my past experience which inhibits a life of celebration. I want to harmonize my heart with your joy-filled heart.

Thank you for your quality of life—the abundant life of Christ which you offer me. I receive it. I lean into the overflowing, abundant life of Christ. And as necessary, I will contend for it.

I'm willing to exercise myself in spiritual warfare to establish a heart of celebration and joy before you.

Heavenly Father, align my relationships. Gather people into my life which stir me to celebrate my life. Help me to do the same for others.

I thank you that joy is significant to you, and that you want it for me.

I will rejoice in you always ...

Amen.

CELEBRATE
WISDOM

Wisdom should be central to our life-pursuit— *"The beginning
of wisdom is this: Get wisdom. Though it cost all you have, get
understanding" (Proverbs 4:7).* The King James Version translates this
verse as *"wisdom is the principal thing."*

Are we after things? Or are we after wisdom?

We can have great confidence because Jesus has become wisdom to us
(see 1 Corinthians 1:30). As we know him more and more, he imparts
his mind to us. Paul said, *"We have the mind of Christ" (1 Corinthians
2:16).*

And here's a wonderful promise from the New Testament— *"If any of you lacks wisdom, you should ask God, who gives generously to all without finding fault, and it will be given to you" (James 1:5).* Ask for it! And start paying attention, because it will come to you in various ways.

An Old Testament word for wisdom includes the meaning of *skillful living*. The Hebraic mindset understood wisdom as a resource to live skillfully, and even artistically. I'm all in for that!

Regulate the Pace of Life

When life is moving too fast ...

> *remember to analyze what got you there ... and fix it!*
>
> *remember to go easy on yourself!*
>
> *remember to eliminate all possible tension points!*
>
> *remember to initiate a change in pace!*
>
> *remember to be even more attentive to relational care!*
>
> *remember to create healthy balance and boundaries!*
>
> *remember that perceived gains will be overshadowed by too many personal losses!*

Call These Things to Mind

Remember this ...

> *insisting on always getting what you want assures that you will never have what you need!*
>
> *lack of discipline is always disastrous!*
>
> *refusing to forgive can never be a final decision!*
>
> *making an effort is always better than making an excuse!*
>
> *arguments based on petty issues are always pretty pathetic!*
>
> *confrontation that is redemptive always works best!*
>
> *sharing your heart is always better than speaking your mind!*

What Can I Do?

I love it when I can do something that leaves me ...

> *deeply aware that the depths of me will never be the same again!*
> *with a very happy heart!*
> *hoping that it never ends!*
> *knowing that I have been greatly blessed!*
> *looking for another opportunity to do it again!*
> *longing for more!*
> *feeling so amazingly good!*

What's Needed

What the world needs now ...

> *is God ... not religion about Him, but relationship with Him ... or so this friend says!*
> *is peace ... lasting peace ... or so the fearful say!*
> *is acceptance ... unconditional acceptance ... or so the rejected say!*
> *is hope ... living hope ... or so the desperate say!*
> *is joy ... real joy ... or so the discouraged say!*
> *is love, sweet love ... or so the song says!*

Staying Power

Some things that never seem to come to an end ...

> *power of love!*
> *sacrifice in serving!*
> *joy in giving!*
> *shocking surprises!*
> *grip of hope!*
> *heart-breaking news!*
> *political positioning!*

Life Lessons from Baseball

Things that frustrated baseball players teach me about life ...

you have to play knowing that others are always watching!

you have to control your emotions!

you have to accept that others impact the rhythm of your game!

you have to play with pain!

you have to take on instruction!

you have to buy in to "team"!

you have to let go of the past and keep playing!

How to Guarantee a Mistake

You always make mistakes when ...

you forgive too slowly!

you do too much!

you plan too little!

you react too harshly!

you speak too soon!

you work too fast!

you judge too quickly!

Insight for Everyone

Here is something everyone should know ...

the only reason why you do not change is ... you!

voices and noises are not silenced by closed doors!

people notice who speaks life and who does not!

being goofy or grumpy never works!

talking over people destroys two great conversations ... at least!

others do pay attention to who finishes first and last ... in almost everything!

What's Needed is Positivity

What we really need is ...

to be sincerely honest about ourselves!

to push beyond frustration to find fulfillment!

to keep accountability directly associated to actions!

to love others as if there is no tomorrow!

to create opportunity not criticize the obstacle!

to live with an open heart and an open hand!

grace to forgive more than guts to fight!

Life Reflection

What are we pursuing?

When God appeared to Solomon and told him to ask for anything and it would be given to him, he asked for wisdom. Because this was his pursuit, God gave him everything else he did not ask for. This is how God is. We can look to Solomon for precedent for our own lives—it's good to follow in the steps of Solomon!

◊ *We live in the so-called Information Age. But we really don't need more information. We need wisdom. What could happen if more people entered the "Wisdom Age?" What could it mean for you, your family, and your work?*

◊ *Ultimately, wisdom is a Person ... God revealed in Jesus Christ. How does this shape your pursuit of wisdom?*

◊ *There are two types of wisdom—wisdom from above and wisdom from below (explore James 3:13-18). For you, what are those channels that convey wisdom from above? And what are those channels that convey wisdom from below?*

◊ *Will you increase your level of request for wisdom?*

◊ *Is the concept of wisdom as the personal capacity to live life skillfully and artistically new to you?*

Prayer & Affirmation

Father, I thank you that wisdom changes everything. I'm grateful that ultimately, wisdom is a Person—your Son, Jesus Christ. I receive Jesus Christ more and more as wisdom for living.

I pray for an increasing measure of the spirit of wisdom and revelation in Christ (see Ephesians 1:17). I receive it. Within that wisdom and revelation is everything I need, now and forever!

I live in wisdom from above, not the wisdom from below. I live and work with extraordinary skill. My life is an expression of art from above. I am God's work of art, "created in Christ Jesus to do good works, which God prepared in advance for us to do" (Ephesians 2:10).

Christ is my wisdom. I have the mind of Christ, so I am open to living with heaven's extraordinary touch!

Amen.

GEMS FOR LIVING

"Things that I know are important ... speaking life, showing kindness and sharing a smile!"
— Terry

Gems are alluring. Captivating. It's understandable that we are drawn to them.

An honest appraisal of those who have merely pursued monetary wealth and gems in this life, reveals to us the bankrupt state of their life-pursuit. It turns out the real gems of life which satisfy are the pursuit of God and his interests, authentic relationships, and facets of wisdom from above.

> *"For where jealousy and selfish ambition exist, there is disorder and every evil thing. But the wisdom from above is first pure, then peaceable, gentle, reasonable, full of mercy and good fruits, unwavering, without hypocrisy" (James 3:16-17).*

Let's build our lives with gold, silver, and precious stones ... not wood, hay, and stubble (see 1 Corinthians 3). We can experience a beautiful life which endures now and forever—a life which God can inhabit.

Be Convinced

I am convinced that ...

>*things get better as we get better!*
>
>*people can feel compassion not just see it!*
>
>*each of us have our own cross to bear!*
>
>*in loving we are loved!*
>
>*it is not bad circumstances that kill us ... it's bad choices!*
>
>*life is ours to embrace and enjoy ... so let's get on with it!*

Routine Is a Friend

The great thing about routine is ...

>*it sets a healthy pace and structures life in a very good way!*
>
>*you can get a lot of things done!*
>
>*you can celebrate the smallest changes!*
>
>*you eliminate a lot of chaos!*
>
>*you keep the main things the main things!*
>
>*you know the rhythm so well!*

What About Today?

What can you do to make today great ...

>*refuse to waste a single moment!*
>
>*let go of issues you cannot resolve!*
>
>*do something that you know will light up someone's world!*
>
>*live in the moment!*
>
>*try to put a smile on the face of everyone you meet!*

leave the past behind!
see the best and celebrate it!

A Good Friend Is Gold

Spending time with a friend ...

so worth it!
always improves the mood you are in!
let the good times begin!
puts a broken heart on the mend!
sharing stories and making memories that never end!
no matter how long you stay together ... you can't wait to meet up again!
my favorite thing to do!

Stay Positively Charged!

Staying positive ...

is easy when you consider the cost of being negative!
keeps you on the up side of life!
helps you be a winner not a whiner!
allows you to make the mundane meaningful!
makes you an inspiration to others!

Don't Be Too Idealistic

Life is bitter, life is sweet ...

so laugh loud, weep willingly ... and give to others generously!
wish I could fix that but I can't!
so in good times or bad ... remember that you never walk alone!
so when life hurts let people help!
so celebrate every sweet day!

sometimes for reasons we cannot understand!
for all of us! Remember that today as you encounter people!

Redeeming the Time

Making the most of every moment ...

the only way to live!
means that we redeem the best out of everything!
that's my plan ... and I hope it is yours!
why live in any other way!
requires us to live in the now!
is much better than every moment making the best of you!

Some Things Important to Me

Things that I know are important ...

speaking life, showing kindness and sharing a smile!
the biggest hurts come from the smallest words!
eating less and moving more!
remembering that you never get a second chance to make a first impression!
doing your best, giving your all and helping those in need!
never waiting until tomorrow to tell someone that you love them!

Everyday Gems

There will be joy in your tomorrows ... wait for it!
There is nothing wrong with having a bad day ... just make sure that in 23 hours and 59 minutes you turn the page!

There will never be a better day than today ... to start doing what you know needs to be done!

There will always be tension in life ... can't have the ying without the yang!

There is no end to learning ... so keep taking notes!

There is potential in every problem we face and in every person we meet ... it's seeing that possibility that is the challenge!

Need a Boost?

When you feel like you need a little boost ...

love extravagantly!

take a walk, grab a nap or my favorite ... have a coffee!

find someone who is hurting and help them!

must do something entirely spontaneous!

talk with a child!

meet with someone who inspires you!

dare to dream again!

Mom Is Right Again

I know you don't want to hear this ...

but your mother was right!

but happiness is a personal choice!

but life is not fair!

but what goes around comes around!

but the other side is not always wrong!

but not everybody is going to like you!

but life is what you make it!

Remember the Best!

When given the opportunity, remember the best about people ...

and do all you can to make it easy for others to remember the best of you!

and hope that others do the same for us!

it shows a heart of mercy!

knowing that people change!

knowing that everyone has to 'live and learn'!

Desperate for Uplifting Words

Words that everyone wants to hear ...

you are the best!

everything will be fine!

it's great to see you!

let me pay for that!

I believe in you!

of course I can help!

Aim for What's Best

Believe for the best ... sometimes experiencing the worst is simply the consequence of not exercising that option!

Whatever keeps us from being our best ... should be the first thing on our list of 'things to deal with'!

Put yourself in the most advantaged place to succeed ... why settle for less than your best!

Believing the best, promoting peace, sharing the struggles ... these are the things that great friends do!

Life Reflection

Consider that "no one can lay any foundation other than the one already laid, which is Jesus Christ" (1 Corinthians 3:11). The person and work of Christ alone can support an enduring life of quality and beauty.

◊ *Jesus said, "Everyone who hears these words of mine and puts them into practice is like a wise man who built his house on the rock" (Matthew 7:24). Is Jesus Christ the true foundation for your life and work?*

◊ *If we're honest, all of us would admit that our lives are a blend of gold, silver, and precious stones ... as well as, wood, hay, and straw. What can you do to start eliminating any wood, hay, and straw you have been building your life with?*

◊ *What can you do to become more intentional about building your life with gold, silver, and precious stones?*

Prayer & Affirmation

Heavenly Father, I praise you for establishing Jesus Christ as a true foundation, an enduring bedrock for authentic living. I embrace Christ as my life-foundation.

I hear the words of Jesus and put them into everyday practice.

Holy Spirit, reveal to me the wood, hay, and straw in my life and work. Help me to see clearly, and increase my resolve to rid my life of it.

Also, reveal to me the gold, silver, and precious stones with which I can build my life. I desire to fulfill my calling with your highest building materials.

All of this is so that my life and work will be a habitation of your presence in this world, Father.

I am the temple of the Spirit's Presence!

Amen.

LIVING YOUR

*"Do all you can, when you can ... do not hold
anything back! In giving all, you gain everything!"*
— Terry

Jesus said, *"Be perfect, therefore, as your heavenly Father is perfect"*
(Matthew 5:48). This seems like an impossible command. What does
it mean?

Jesus is not saying we will come to a place in our journey where we
won't make mistakes. And it certainly does not mean that we will not
need the grace of God ... not only to cleanse us of sins and failure, but
also to empower us to live according to our full potential.

The word perfect in this verse means *complete* or *whole.* Jesus invites
us into wholeness. We can live with personal integrity. Our lives can be
complete, not partial.

When we're born again, and begin to follow Jesus, we are re-qualified to live our best life. The life-force of Jesus empowers us to be our best self.

As we live in alignment with our best self, we live a life of integrity. Remember, integrity is power. Integrity accelerates our life and work, harmonizing our personal experience with the design of heaven!

It starts with this: resolve afresh every day, week, and year to be your best self! And then consistently ask for grace to empower your life.

You Effect Change

Every action has a corresponding reaction ...

> *so we have to monitor and measure always!*
>
> *so we do need to hold that thought!*
>
> *so what worked for Newton works for us!*
>
> *so no surprises here!*
>
> *so actually we decide first how things are going to go!*
>
> *so we have to give what we want to get back!*
>
> *so before we act, we have to think about that!*

Creativity Makes the Difference

Thinking creatively ...

> *a skill that is needed now more than ever!*
>
> *adds value to every discussion, process and organization!*
>
> *nurtures a positive attitude!*
>
> *means thinking beyond ... in every way!*
>
> *is truly a team thing!*
>
> *makes many things possible that others have called impossible!*
>
> *thinking creatively ... is something that we can train ourselves to do!*

Maximize Opportunity

When given the opportunity to help ...

always do only what you can!

make a difference, not a dent!

think development, not betterment!

remember that what is requested may not be what is required!

say "yes" ... then figure out what is best!

Grace is Empowerment

Choosing to be a "grace-filled" person ...

can anything be better!

commits us to embrace value-based realities!

corrects our perspective and position!

contributes to positive development in every way!

confirms that we will be a great add to any person or process!

creates opportunity and opens doors!

causes life and hope to flourish!

Live from the Inside Out

Progressive personal development ...

is noticed by everyone!

keeps a pathway of opportunity open!

without it destiny is at risk!

is always a personal choice!

assures that you will remain proactive, not reactionary!

keeps the dream alive!

saves you from the tyranny of delayed regret!

Crystal Clear Clarity

In order to communicate clearly ...

seek to do it better!

slow down, take the time to say it well!

shed some light ... illustrate to make it clear!

speak to your listener ... do not pontificate!

show respect for the gap ... the communication gap I mean!

stay focused until you get it said!

say only what needs to said ... and then stop!

Today is the Day

Encounter God's activity in the NOW ...

Preparation promotes possibilities ... it seems that good things happen more often for those who live ready!

Never assume that the good that could be done, the changes that could be made, or the encouraging words that could be spoken have happened!

In reality all we have that we can actually make ours is ... today!

Celebrate every moment, cherish every memory ... live with no regrets!

Making the most of every moment is simply a personal choice ... either "Yes, I will," or, "No, I won't!"

Live today as if there is no tomorrow ... that's the simplest way I know to get my best effort every day!

Delay brought on by disobedience only breeds disappointment ... and ultimately brings on disaster!

The secret for seeing results ... is to start now and stay with it!

Now ... is all we have ... this present moment! Redeem it fully while it is still in your hands!

There is no joy in living for yesterday ... only the assurance that you will be disappointed in today!

Living with a Possibility Mentality

All things are possible with God ... and with you when you're with God!

> *If we say "yes", then nothing can stop us ... if we say "no", then nothing can save us!*

> *Challenges always come with choices ... they either produce crisis or promote creativity! Choose creativity!*

> *Success does not come because we know how to talk the talk ... it comes when we begin to walk the talk!*

> *At the end of the day, it is your attitude not your appearance, that makes you most attractive ... so be smart and take care of your heart!*

> *Remember ... the prized value in the 'development process' is participation ... not completion! Staying engaged is key!*

> *When the future seems fuzzy .. look only for the next step, not the next stage! It's amazing how things will clear up and come together!*

> *When there is no reasonable explanation as to why things are going wrong ... the only real answer is to craft a 'radical solution'! You have to stop pondering and go proactive!*

> *Get in ... give all ... gain everything! That pretty much describes passionate-living and the price for winning!*

> *Hopeful expectation is a beautiful thing! It allows you to dream again and causes your heart to sing!*

> *When facing a mountain of problems ... don't moan ... get motivated!*

> *Pray, prioritize, process if necessary ... but take on the task! That's the only way through!*

Press Forward with Passion

Life is designed to be lived with passion!

> *When you can't get your heart into something, it is really best to get your hands off of it ... as soon as possible!*

> *So what is keeping you from being your best today? In the time it takes to describe it ... you could deal with it!*

There are many created 'refining' moments ... where deep things happen ... like when passion meets patience for example! ... That will test you for sure ... I know!

Shift your position, stir your passion, sharpen your perspective ... you will love what you feel!

The push forward is a much better option than the pull downward! Journey on!

Provoking a passionate heart is easy ... reaching a cynical critic is exhausting! Be willing to do the hard work!

Do all you can, when you can ... do not hold anything back! In giving all you gain everything!

People are a Priority

We always lose when we undervalue people. We win when we make them a priority.

Funerals have a way of making you realize that every person is special in their own way ... so remember the best of people!

People are precious ... and sadly it is often only after they are gone that we realize that!

Try to see their value now rather than later!

Nothing is better than having the time and opportunity to celebrate a great friendship!

Celebrate every moment ... because each one is special, and in adding value, you make them significant!

There is nothing greater than a committed friend! You can't really describe the depth of their caring ... or define the depth of their contribution!

Music soothes my soul, friends and family warm my heart and the love of God sweetens my spirit! When these things are present I am at peace!

Loving and being loved is the most powerful reality in the world! When love is present the world makes sense!

The voice of a friend awakens the joy within ... and your world becomes a better place because of that grace! Be that voice today!

A great friendship is not costly ... it's an investment! It always pays you back more than you give!

If you want to generate good ideas ... be a thinker! But if you want to gather great ideas ... be a team player!

Advancing Forward with Mission

Work hard, play hard, rest hard.

Remember that all work and no play is a bad idea ... not even healthy for you!

The things that are planted deep in your heart will become the 'issues of life' that determine what you do and who you will become!

Things feeling a little chaotic ... it may be time to shut down and reconfigure!

Wish we could copy and paste life lessons rather than having to learn them one by one!

When you need to work fast ... expect delays! It will help ... in life and with computers!

Process well all the things that are in your hands and plan well for all the things that are in your head!

Remember ... computers are not the only things that need a 'reboot' now and then!

When you feel that you have too much to do ... pause a bit, plunge in ... then you can put a plan in place to fix it!

Life Reflection

Within our hearts, we all have a deep-seated instinct to live our best life. This is part of the Grand Design.

◊ *Jesus said, "Be perfect as the Father is perfect." Have you thought of this statement as unattainable? How does appreciating the word "perfect" in this verse as meaning "complete" or "whole" enhance your understanding of Jesus' saying?*

◊ *On a scale of 1 to 10, how have you been doing with this concept: Jesus is interested in you living your best life? Or, has your thinking been more like, "I'm saved. I'm desperate. And thank God I'll one day go to heaven!"*

◊ *We're designed to live powerful lives. Personal integrity (your best life) = personal empowerment. How does this make you feel? Offended? Excited? Surprised? Relieved?*

Prayer & Affirmation

Heavenly Father, I exalt you for your excellencies. You are a God of design, beauty, and function.

I fully accept Jesus' saying that I am to be perfect as You are perfect. I will be whole. I will be complete. I say with firm faith: "Christ is consummate completeness! And I am complete in Christ!" Hallelujah!

I am born again. I am a follower of Christ, an apprentice of His Kingdom. As such, I have been re-qualified to live my best life—a life in harmony with my new nature in Christ.

Old things have passed away. All things are becoming new!

I live a life of authentic power. No substitutes!. I will not settle. Christ, may you receive the reward of your suffering in my life. Through my life!

Father, I will live with all of my heart. And all for your Glory, and Your Story. Consume me with Your zeal! In the name of Christ the Lord,

Amen.

WHAT'S NEEDED IS
LEADERSHIP

"Efficient leaders know exactly what they want to do, why they want to do it and how they will get it done." — Terry

Leadership affects everything. But what does authentic leadership look like?

James and John asked Jesus if they could sit on his right and left hand in the glory of his Kingdom! As the other 10 disciples became indignant, Jesus called them together.

"You know that those who are regarded as rulers of the Gentiles lord it over them, and their high officials exercise authority over them. Not so with you. Instead, whoever wants to become great among you must be your servant, and whoever wants to be first must be slave of all. For even the Son of Man did not come to be served, but to serve, and to give his life as a ransom for many" (Mark 10:42-45).

Jesus demonstrated that leading is loving and serving. It's the laying down of one's life for others ... and for a cause greater than one's personal interests.

You may say, *"I'm not a leader."* Yes, you are. You are providing a lead on something. There may not be an official title or position, but you are offering leadership to someone, to something. Consider that Jesus was not too big on titles and public recognition anyway!

What's needed today is quality leadership! Leadership ensures that the right things happen. What are you designed to lead?

Please Give Us Real Leadership!

Real leadership is remarkable.

> *Leaders don't explain our troubles to us and then criticize others who they claim are to blame for it all ... leaders embrace the troubles!*
>
> *Efficient leaders know exactly what they want to do, why they want to do it and how they will get it done!*
>
> *Effective leaders know how to communicate clearly to others!*
>
> *Heads up leaders everywhere ... people are looking to see your example, not to hear your excuses!*
>
> *Great leaders do more than solve problems and make bold decisions ... they craft amazing solutions and create environments of success!*
>
> *Be the kind of leader who can create incredible momentum out of an inspired moment!*

Leaders Process the Possibilities

Quality leadership creates opportunities for the best things to happen!

> *All of us love talking about possibilities and progress ... but the 'process' discussion ... well, that seems to be the one we all try to avoid!*
>
> *Frustration is just wasted energy unless it forces you to find a solution ... so push on! Our world needs winners not whiners!*
>
> *I am amazed by the great tragedies that some people have to overcome to win ... and by the small things that cause others to quit!*

Love seeing the developmental process at work ... wherever it is taking place!

Personal growth, organizational progress and positive changes are such exciting experiences!

In a world that seems to be increasingly filled with doubters and distractors ... we need to be dreamers and doers!

When life stretches you to your limits, remember ... that is the plan! It is only then that we discover new depths of potential and possibility!

Catching momentum is much easier than creating it ... so I have work to do!

Love new opportunities and the energy they create!

Today will offer both obstacles and opportunities—fix the obstacles but focus on the opportunities!

Funny how great opportunities and huge challenges are almost constant companions! I am on my way to enjoy (?) both!

The Significance of the Leader's Interior Life

There's no escaping it—we lead from the inside out.

Moments of reflection are powerfully important for us ... because they enable us to renew perspective, reestablish priorities, refocus purpose and refresh passion!

If we make today a time of contemplation, then tomorrow will be a better day of celebration!

Wisdom is not a possession ... it's a partnership!

Unconditional love, unshakable hope, undisturbed peace ... absolute acceptance, perfect promises, full forgiveness!

The longing of hope lingers in every heart ... seen or unseen ... it's always there ... so share hope!

In reality, 'perspective' should be based on informed observation ... not biased individual opinion! It seems we need to push the 'reset' button!

Hope only needs a spark of inspiration and then .. all by itself it will create a life of its own ... in any situation! Inspire hope today!

Not everything seen needs to be said ... not everything heard needs to be held ... but everything forgiven needs to be forgotten!

There is a hope that will endure no matter how dark the night!

When you are a hope-giver, the world always greets you with a smile!

Seeing the good, believing the best and hoping for more are increasingly difficult things to do ...

... and yet they remain as the essential elements of a grateful heart, so they still call out to us, especially now!

Beyond the troubles there is still plenty to be thankful for ... so count those things one by one!

When I think about all the things I have to be thankful for ... I wonder why I whine so much at times? That's gotta change!

The Leader in Community with Others

Real leaders are not alone. They are rightly connected with others.

I will spend today reconnecting with special friends ... as good as it gets for me!

Celebrating with a friend is the main thing on my 'to do list' today! I love days like this!

Unhealthy relationships are ridiculously ugly and unyielding in what they require ... so the only real option is to be unconditional in your love and uncompromising in your awareness of your own limitations!

Our words either bless people or bring them down ... pretty simple huh? So how are the people in your world going to fare today?

I value my friends, and you know why? If you are rich in friends you will never feel poor ... no matter what!

Being a friend matters to me!

I lost a great friend and am reminded again that great friends are irreplaceable—so when death forces you to live on the memories, it's still OK!

I'm staying connected, because relationships matter!

There's nothing better than belonging to a spiritual community that you long to be with! Why just 'go to church'?

A true friend never gets in your way unless you happen to be going down!

I value relational connections!

Building community is a actually a matter of building bridges!

Walking together and staying close in good times and bad ... that's the kind of friend I need and want to be!

I'm reminded again that staying close to people really matters! Never give up or let go!

Being with people gives me energy! Good thing considering what I do!

I know the importance of being focused ... but also the necessity of having fun! Now that explains a lot!

A friend who really listens and truly cares ... now there's a life treasure!

I am often in situations where the diversity seems to dictate that meaningful connection is impossible, and yet, love always finds a way!

Resolving conflict is as much about relational concern as it is giving the right counsel!

A big part in being happy about what you do ... is being happy with you!

I seriously have great friends ... so impressed with who they are and what they do!

I know we must remain 'first generation' in the heart, but I love the heritage of 'generational faith'!

I'm connecting leaders because relationships matter!

Quality Leaders are Effective Communicators

Quality leadership advances people and situations with effective, fruitful communication.

Lack of clarity, compassion, connection and cultural understanding in our communication is at the root of every relational crisis!

Clear, consistent, compassionate communication is a critical skill to develop!

Finding the right words at the right time is not that easily done ... but really powerful when it happens!

Funny how what you intend to say is not actually what gets communicated! Oh, yeah there is a story here!

Quality Leaders Exhibit Strength

Extraordinary strength radiates from extraordinary leaders.

Unless the place you are standing in has a long history (like eternal) of being solid, then you need to always be ready for sudden shifts!

Nothing better than starting what will be a very busy day early, with lots of energy and expectation!

When life moves too fast, we really only have two choices ... run to catch up or create a new rhythm ... and wait for life to catch on!

Well, I am off ... with a killer daily plan in hand! If all goes well, this will be one very productive day!

The challenge of course is not in describing life ... but in defining it!

Because the choices we make will have deep and enduring impact on so many ... we need to make smart, safe, selfless choices!

In reality, every heart wants to dream ... so dare people to dream, knowing that a heart that believes the best can survive the worst!

Changes, challenges and concerns ... constant companions, so be ready for them!

Making a decision at the right time is as important as making the right decision! Remembering this principle is critical!

Now more than ever, we need to share all the good news we can share, salute all the good guys we can salute and show all the goodness we can show!

Encouraging people to dream again is a wonderful gift!

Need to quieten the chaos in your life ... refocus on the principles that guide your life, rather than the pressures that drive the moment!

Nothing better than finding new strength ... especially when you know that new challenges await!

Do I have an opportunity or an obstacle in front of me ... it's my choice that decides that, not the circumstances!

Today is just one of those 'roll up your sleeves and take it on' kind of day for me!

It is always best to take on the challenge of the day! If not, it becomes a problem tomorrow!

First you dream it, then you do it ... that's why I love planning!

Life Reflection

What can you provide a lead on? What need or opportunity is not being addressed ... perhaps until you step up? Are you willing to love? Are you ready to serve? Are you willing to pay the price of authentic leadership to advance what is good and true?

◊ *Have you thought of yourself as a leader? If not, is there anything in your past, or in your interior world, that may be holding you down? Will you face these issues for the sake of others, for the sake of Christ and his Kingdom?*

◊ *Perhaps you are a leader now ... you may even have a title and official position. How is it going? Is there any way in which you have yielded to the temptation to use leadership for your own personal ends (recognition, control, personal advancement)? If so, are you ready to change and truly follow Jesus' model of leadership?*

◊ *Look around your personal world. Where is leadership needed from your vantage point? What are the two or three things that immediately come to mind? Are you willing to stand in these spaces?*

Prayer & Affirmation

Heavenly Father,

What are you up to? What do you want to do in your world?

What's happening on earth that needs to stop? What's not happening that needs to start? Is there anything you want me to provide a lead on for your Dream? Show me. Show me in any way you want to.

Holy Spirit, teach me to lay down my life. Inspire me to serve as Jesus served. I affirm that the world's ways are not my model for leadership. Jesus is my Mentor, my Life Coach.

Father, I'm willing to step out and step up. I don't need a title. I don't crave an official position. I don't long for the accolades of people. I just want to do what I'm designed to do. I'm willing to provide leadership in ways which are not under the bright lights. I'll lead for an Audience of One.

I'm excited! I'll lead with zeal and diligence moving forward (Romans 12:8).

All for you, Father. For your people. For your world.

Amen.

Afterword

This book, *Whispered Wisdom To Live Beyond,* is a collection of quotes and sayings that I have created, and I want you to know why they have been written.

As a young man, I slowly came to understand the realities of destiny, and in that discovery process there was, deep within me, a desire to be an effective communicator.

I clearly remember reading books, or hearing speakers and being captivated, not only by their content, but also by their creative literary style.

I longed to be able to say things that were eloquently spoken in ways that would capture the hearers and communicate to them in a manner that was accurate and appropriate. I fell in love with Proverbs 25:11, *"A word fitly spoken is like apples of gold in settings of silver."*

It was this prompting that provoked me to write something every day to be published ... and I felt compelled to tag those words with *"ASCOLTA"* ... my tagline of choice.

This book is just a first gleaning of what has been written ... there is a volume of quotes and sayings to be published ... and I am still writing!

My life and literary aim remains the same ...

"With all the creativity that God will grant me, I will spend all of my days creating a life and crafting words that will inspire, encourage and provoke all those who come to know them, to choose to live beyond themselves, fully committed to making a difference."

This is what pleasures my heart and the heart of my God ... and in this my joy is complete!

Terry Hoggard

About the Author

Terry and his family have been European missionaries since 1984, serving for almost ten years in Rome, Italy as the founding pastor of International Christian Fellowship. He served as the Senior Pastor of Brussels Christian Center in Brussels, Belgium from 1995-2005.

Terry currently serves as Relational Leader of Global International Church Network, which he launched in 2012 (www.globalicn.com) and as a coach

Terry and Ruthanne

and consultant for Fellowship Of European International Churches (www.feic.org), a network that he founded in 2004. He serves with AGWM European Leadership Team, engaging in several networking initiatives including leading the Development Team for Continental Theological Seminary in Brussels. Terry serves with the leadership team of International Christian Fellowship in Malmo, Sweden (www.icfeuropaporten.se) and Accenture Christian Fellowship.

Terry is a certified life coach who engages progressive leaders to co-create a change process that will inspire better performance at every level.

"I have spent a lifetime building relationships, nurturing life-giving connections, creating teams, resolving conflict and seeking to make a difference. These are the things that make my heart sing and because of that I have engaged in some very exciting opportunities that have prepared me to serve you well."

www.globalicn.com
www.feic.org

www.ingramcontent.com/pod-product-compliance
Lightning Source LLC
Chambersburg PA
CBHW061150040426
42445CB00013B/1641

9 7 8 0 6 9 2 4 1 7 9 6 6